Species

by

Jessica L Conley

Finishing Line Press
Georgetown, Kentucky

Species

Copyright © 2025 by Jessica L Conley
ISBN 979-8-88838-913-3 First Edition
All rights reserved under International and Pan-American Copyright Conventions. No part of this book may be reproduced in any manner whatsoever without written permission from the publisher, except in the case of brief quotations embodied in critical articles and reviews.

ACKNOWLEDGMENTS

I am grateful to the readers and editors of the following publications in which versions of these poems first appeared:

Poetry South: "The Amniocentesis"
Common Ground Review: "La Personne"
2River: "The Women All Wear Black Dresses"
Exit 7: "Shelf Road," "Driving Past 8720 River Road on Christmas," and "Grocery Shopping After School"
Moida: "Eternal Cycle: A Peaceful Mind"
Alternating Current Press: "Imprinting"
Wingless Dreamer: "The Volunteers"
glassworks: "Falcon 9"

I would like to thank my husband John R. Conley for supporting my passions, for fact-checking my musical allusions, and for inspiring me every day.

Thank you to my aunt Tah Madsen, whose beautiful artwork is featured on the cover of this collection.

Thank you to my advisor and friend Gregory Donovan for encouraging me to write and be the artist I have dreamed of being, as well as all of my peers and professors at Virginia Commonwealth University from whom I have learned so much–Kathleen Graber and David Wojahn in particular. I appreciate your time and careful attention to my work.

Publisher: Leah Huete de Maines
Editor: Christen Kincaid
Cover Art: Tah Madsen
Author Photo: John R. Conley
Cover Design: Elizabeth Maines McCleavy

Order online: www.finishinglinepress.com
also available on amazon.com

Author inquiries and mail orders:
Finishing Line Press
PO Box 1626
Georgetown, Kentucky 40324
USA

Contents

I
Species 1
La Personne 3
Summer 4
Anti-Elegy Wearing a Wrinkled Scarf 5
Eternal Cycle: Hanna's World 7
Shelf Road 8
A Row of Skirts 9
Self-Portrait with Child 11
Eternal Cycle: Sorciere! 12
Poem for the Transcriber of My Household Captioned Telephone 13
Miramar Plays 14

II
What to Wear to a Fuck Cancer Party 17
Covered 18
Autumn 19
The Women All Wear Black Dresses 20
November of My Tenth Year 21
Hay Song 22
Eternal Cycle: A Child's Dream 23
Still Life (An Offering) 24
The Amniocentesis 25
At World Market You and I Shop for a Living Room Carpet 26
Eternal Cycle: Nomad's Dance 28
After You Died, I Looked for Your Poem 29
Anti-Elegy Before the First Frost 30

III
Soul Theory Cast in Bronze 35
Recollection Following a Rest 36
Winter 38
Aubade from the Stokesville Country Store Parking Lot in February 39

Self-Portrait on the Surface of Someone Else 40
Imprinting 42
Tat Tvam Asi (You Are That) 44
Anti-Elegy with a Nine Iron in Its Hand 45
Looking Glass Falls... 46
Eternal Cycle: A New Life 48
Driving Past 8720 River Road on Christmas 50
Eternal Cycle: Back to the Light 51

IV
Long Ago Was the Then Beginning to Seem Like Now 55
Grocery Shopping After School... 56
Spring... 58
Eternal Cycle: A Peaceful Mind... 59
Kenny Werner on the One-Finger Piano Exercise that Opens
    the Door to God 60
The Volunteers 61
Falcon 9.. 62
Anti-Elegy with a Painter's Brush and a Bowl of Unripe Peaches 63
Eternal Cycle: Terre des Hommes 65
Burial Mounds (The New Year).. 66

The only rules demanding the interdependence of contrapuntal voices are these: that the voices should meet at certain points in comprehensible harmonies, and that together they should distinctly express the tonality. Otherwise they should be as independent as possible.

—Arnold Schoenberg, "First Species" from *Preliminary Exercises in Counterpoint*

The title, *Terre des Hommes,* could be translated as "land of men," or "mankind's earth." This album is to me an impressionist piece. It transcribes the way I feel towards life, earth, mankind, philosophy, spirituality, science… a soundtrack for your imagination.

—Stephane Wrembel, notes on his album *Terre des Hommes*

I

Species

> *Species, a type of musical counterpoint, is the layering of multiple melodies and which incorporates dissonant tones.*

I prefer Miles Davis on the flugelhorn and listen to the same

album *Miles Ahead*
over and over
in my car, knowing

which song is next, how each solo will end and return.

I tell John to leave
the door open
when he practices.

I straighten our wedding photo, askew from the metronome's *doom*,

clack, clack, clack.
We're all trying
to be better. I envy

the way he plays in time yet allows space before the next

note's arrival,
knows which rules
to abandon,

which to keep. In theory, there is only one way to end

a fourth species
counterpoint: *re, do.*
What's the meaning

of the blues without flute and French horn? I drive to meet him

at the Chesapeake
Bay on Thanksgiving
eve. Hearing

The Beatles—*You won't see me*—from the driveway, I walk to

the back deck and
slide the glass door,

I'm here. John

and his mother are shucking oysters and singing by the open

grill. The shells clink
to the ground—one half,
then the other.

La Personne

My grandmother and her friends used to call each other to make sure
they were still alive. I am terrified of being old, forgetting
what I did last week, & relying on someone to help me up the stairs.
Of living too long but not forever. Of no one answering the phone.

To say person in French, *personne*. To say no one, *personne*,
like recalling the body that made the absence,
like existing without the body—personne, one day posing as me;
tomorrow, eternal. *Personne* without shadows, full of light,
always leaving for something, for nothing, *rien*.
I miss her desperately.

I used to want to be that *personne*, empty, undying—
one who has never gone shopping for butter and brown sugar,
never slit her finger cutting open a squash,
never had someone clean her wound before wrapping it with gauze,
never had someone look into her eyes and ask, *Better*?

Summer

With the ground still damp from days of rain, I spend
the morning weeding scutch grass
from the gravel walkways,
twirling wiry roots around my forefinger, reaching for the rootstalk,
pulling rhizomes that hold deep into the rock.
The yard is soft with late summer.

Bell peppers, dark with rings of rot. Zucchini blossoms,
matted like folded napkins.
Tomatoes, splitting their seams.
Jalapenos, white with stretch marks. I grasp and pull
what spreads from the center, line up what I can salvage
along the windowsill.
I've seen this harvest before.

Along the bar were nearly empty glasses and folded paper
napkins wet with rings
from wine. Late summer was soft in the room
where Anthony Wilson's quartet played, musicians
sweating through their shirts. The pianist stood,
leaned over the grand piano's keys, reaching his hands beneath—
beyond the hammers—
to strum the open strings.

Anti-Elegy Wearing a Wrinkled Scarf

> *Watch the turmoil of beings,*
> *but contemplate their return....*
> *You can deal with whatever life brings you,*
> *and when death comes, you are ready.*
> —Tao Te Ching

The clothes iron, below folded fabrics of diaphanous sky,
smooths rust-colored plains. Steam—or is it mist

rising from the falls?—blurs the river's border
of Carl Warner's *Tefal Clothescape.* Where are its seams,

its stitches, its source? Whoever abandoned this world,
leaving tea towels of snow on wrinkled heaps,

must have tired of tending it all.
I flip over the clothescape postcard you've sent me,

read about your recent ski trips: Vail, twice.
Late February, driving home from Breckenridge

in a blizzard, you could not even see the road.

According to the Tao, *Each separate being in the universe*
returns to the common source. I have emptied

my mind. Or so I thought. There it is again, a portmanteau
of scarves and mountains.

What a mess. Sometimes I press my evening
dresses and order takeout, binge watch *Project Runway*.

This morning as I washed dishes, I imagined you:
already buckling your ski boots, having already

traced a blue route with your finger—*Lower Forget-Me-Not*
to *Northstar*. One more load of laundry

and this landscape would be too full, rivers flooded,
roads buried. On the return drive in the snow,

you followed the taillights in front of you.

I will never be ready, you wrote. *When I got home,
I couldn't stop shaking.*

Eternal Cycle: Hanna's World

after Stephane Wrembel's album Terre Des Hommes

Consider the cyclamen after it blooms / how its summer slumber resembles death / yellowed leaves dropping / as though they will never / again drink light / When Ravel composed *Pavane pour une infante défunte* / people wondered / who the child was / the sad story of her death / though Ravel wrote the title / simply for love / of the sound / So in English / we've named it / Pavane for a Dead Princess / There is no princess / no life / no death / no child I want / to name / Hanna / who steps legato / to the pianist's study of overlapping hands / sequins stitched in her sweater / hands crossing over pearled notes / *La fille n'a pas la fin* / Hanna / born from song / ready to rebloom / the girl alive / on a winter evening / dancing

Shelf Road

    for Rachel

When I visited you in Colorado last summer   after your fall
we chose an out-and-back   along the washes below Cactus Cliff
      We heard   *I'm safe*   in the distance and turned to watch
a climber's open hands grip the cliff's surface that glinted its steel
bones at the sky   You said   *I'm so bombarded*
by epic shit   and I thought you must have been thinking about
the hangboard you've left untouched   The ground was far
from the climber's feet   In an archeology of fear
the climber hammered the next piton into the rock   To the south
Shelf Road scarred through Piñon pine like the pale line of a fossilized
invertebrate   We had hours to hike the reef of the ancient
lagoon   dry washed in heat and black limestone
Your hair would have cracked if you had brushed it   You stopped
to re-braid it in knots   We ate the avocados you packed
warm and soft on the whole wheat crackers   walked further from
where the climber was rappelling   running backwards
into a familiar fall *He must be tired*   I supposed   You looked away
from the cliff's plate of bones   Together   we hiked
the Pierre shale's fractures and sutures   You picked a juniper berry
with your thumb and forefinger   held it for me
to smell the cypress
     held its life with just two fingers

A Row of Skirts

    for my mother

Wind gathers under your down parka
as you walk in the snow along State Street—

that's how I picture you
on your way to your favorite store

to inspect skirt fabric designs—

metallic gold or rubbed sage, scattered roses
like a dropped eyeshadow palette?

—selecting silk chiffon whose color shattered
beautifully, unconcerned its pattern mimics another's.

Ever since you moved away

to the city of Anish Kapoor's *Cloud Gate*,
I open your packages days before my birthday,

peeking through cracks in the wrapping.
Your note is pleated in tissue: *Thought of you.*

*

Your note—*Thought of you*—
peeks through cracks in the wrapping.

Each year, I open my gift days before my birthday
then lie to you & say I waited.

Ever since you returned to the city of Cloud Gate,
seven years of skirts palindrome my closet.

You buy what you find
beautiful, unconcerned its pattern mimics another's,

selecting silk chiffon whose color shattered
like a dropped eyeshadow palette.

You inspect fabric for softness
delicately, the way I picture you:

you walk in the snow along State Street,
wind gathering under your down parka.

Self-Portrait with Child

Aubrey selects a PAW Patrol
coloring page for me,
gives herself a blank sheet.

I ask, *What are you drawing?*
She replies, *I don't know.*
I'm not done. With each press
of her markers to the page,
she makes more of her world
in which limbs connect
to hearts and sunflowers
bloom from shoes. Washable

Crayola colors are strewn
across the table. With her fist
clutching the one she has chosen,
she works to compose
a girl with cloud-like hair
and large eyes. She will not

stop for her snack of yogurt
and cherries until she
is finished. She rubs a drying
purple across the landscape
behind herself then pushes
the paper to the side,

examines my Dalmatian
wearing a fire hat, and uses
what is left of her marker
to fill in his tag. As for the pile
of paper remaining, she stands
on her stool to grab us each
a clean, blank page—
there is so much left to do.

Eternal Cycle: Sorciere!

The concierge walks each row of each tier
at the Théâtre des Champs-Élysées, collecting
programs from the floor, marking chairs

to be reupholstered. As he moves on to the stage,
picking up the triangle beater left in haste,
he replays the afternoon performance,

Stravinsky's *Le Sacre du printemps*,
in his mind, gauging the moment the audience
began to moan, then stand, then scream, beat upon

the heads of those near in that rhythm
of Part II, scene ii, the circle of ballerinas stomping
in crescendo. Though it was not, he remembers,

until the *Glorification de l'élue*—the sonority
of inconstant time, accented slurs and pizzicato
heard barbaric—that the politician in the second row

bit his wife's ear. The concierge had stayed
for the final movement—the center puppet-ballerina,
her arms' and neck's fatal grace, entranced him.

He had never seen, had never heard,
a woman dancing to her death. He did not turn,
could not leave, even as the audience shoved him,

tried to force him through the side doors.
Now, after his shift has ended, he walks home
along the riverbank, noticing how the boats pitch

in the pulse of the Seine, how his shoes knock
against the cobbled streets, how stark
the branches of forsythia wild, composing yellow.

Poem for the Transcriber of My Household Captioned Telephone

after Joseph Millar's "Telephone Repairman"

All evening, in the muted
television's flickering light,
my husband talks to his mother
on our captioned telephone, reading
the words you are transcribing—
hello becomes *hello,*
goodnight, I love you becomes *goodnight, I love you—*
so that he may hear them as they are,
from her mouth into the wire.

You adjust your headphones to better
listen to her speak, shape
her voice into script, line after line:
You should come visit. I'll make the guest bed.
Maybe next week,
phrases that hesitate,
you wanting to be sure of the words.

When the days are too loud—
the churn of our old
washing machine, the blare
of a fire truck—he leaves his hearing
aides in their case, untroubled
by silence. We live so much of our lives without
speaking, he and I touching
the soil to tell if one of us
has already watered the garden,
him taping a note to the coffee pot, *the plumber*
is coming between 11-4.

You can hear the many sounds
stirring within her, from the mother to her son,
and surely you wonder
how to type her sighing in reply,
her breath filling whole measures,
speaking in the voice he knows.

Miramar Plays "Por Siempre"

A woman waves from the back of the venue.
So often I find myself squinting in the dark while an organ
whirrs with notes that refuse to let go of their beginning.

Karen, over the clack of the claves, says, *My friend Lena.*
After the singer introduces her next bolero,
I compliment Lena's necklace, its pendant the color of fava

bean and shaped like the moon's orbit resting
just below her collar bones. A sculptor told Lena to choose it
from a wall of Sicilian clay shapes. She took the one

that represents her life, the one that fit the contour
of her hand. As Miramar plays "Por Siempre,"
Lena unfastens her necklace. I think I hear

her say I should hold it. It is heavier than I expected.
The organ's chords signal the set is ending. I do not believe in it,
but I love songs about *forever:*

a man who lives beside Moonshine Creek tends to seven barren
Fraser fir speckled with twig gouting. I told him

it was good, what he was doing. We squinted in the dusk
at the browning needles high above our heads.

II

What to Wear to a Fuck Cancer Party

A green skirt with blue velvet stars and ankle boots and gold

        bicycle earrings with hearts as wheels

It's Dia de los Muertos

Mark & Tracy have repainted their stucco house

        green like moss embalmed

At the entrance is the ofrenda full of photos and burning candles

        to honor those who have died of cancer this year and last

For the occasion Tracy has dressed

        the dining room table in tortillas and roses

I fill my plate with tamales de huitlacoche & mole verde con tofu

We listen to Mirabel tell a story of being stuck in the snow

        and the procession

        of characters who helped tow out her car

        the FedEx driver who scattered salt on the hillside

        the bridesmaids who pushed in French heels

I eat another tamale

        spill roasted poblano cream on the hem of my pink blouse

Next to me pictures of dead friends with frosting

        on their faces and sparklers in their hands

        awake to marigolds

        and the candle flames stealing down their wicks

Covered

Each morning, once awake, I pull my spirit from the sound well
and wash my face with lemongrass
soap. *Good morning, I love you*
the same	as yesterday's *Good morning,*
I love you. Another finch pecks at rotting leaves
in the gutters. Brown flecks
flutter down. I cut ripe pineapple from its core. Yesterday, I poured
a glass of grapefruit juice—viscous, tidal—and listened
to birds and cicadas
on their endless loop. Sometimes, it can all feel new,
like the way Brandi Carlile covered "Take Me Home, Country Roads"
at Maymont Park the summer	after the super blue
blood moon.
		Toward the end,
a stranger put her palm on my hip, rested her forehead
on the back of my neck, humming,
To the place I belong, beer spilling on my sandals.
I turned to her	in the dark, and she stepped back,
surprised, mumbled, *Sorry, I didn't see.*
In the moment before her eyes met mine, I wanted something more
than her thinking I was	someone else.

Autumn

> *But were some child of yours alive that time,*
> *You should live twice, in it, and in my rhyme.*
> *—William Shakespeare, Sonnet 17*

Last night, a windstorm felled trees across a power
line. I woke to the clock blinking

a constellation. Electricity passing through a bulb
expresses as light. Night is nothing

other than night. By the lake, beavers chew trees
into hour glasses. While I slice radishes

into moon halos for a salad,
Ricky Skaggs plays from my iPod

in a pint glass. Holding the knife,
I see my mother's hands in mine—the wrinkles

at our knuckles, the veins beneath
our freckles. One person's hands must be

another's eternal life. Beyond my window, the wind
scatters golden. Leaves fall and have fallen.

The Women All Wear Black Dresses

The women all wear black dresses
and wide-brimmed black hats with bouquets,
netting, and silk bows. Some chickens sit
on their laps, others are grasped
more tightly, black and white-rippled
feathers jutting between women's fingers.
If it were not a photograph, in a moment,
the women in the front row would stand,
birds scattering in false flight.
On the bottom corner,
written in cursive, *Hen Party 1937*—
it's one of those old family photographs;
there's no one left who knows,
so my mother and I make up their stories:

That's Lara smoothing the wreath of dark
feathers at her chicken's neck, and great-aunt
Julia with the Orpington is mid-story,
telling Phyllis's sister about her broody hen.
Phyllis (who was almost late because she
couldn't find her crocheted gloves)
describes how she dunks her hen
in cold water to make it abandon its nest.
My mother and I like this reunion
with family we never knew we lost. They wear
subtle smiles, glad to be known, mud
and feathers about their skirts. In the back,
two boys, slouched and squinting, sit atop
a fence, waiting for something to be over.

November of My Tenth Year

Handprint turkeys decorate the fridge
of the small, blue house.
Water boils in a thin tin pot
rattling on the stove.
My grandfather mistakes it for rain
and leans back in his rocking chair
to look outside toward the woods
where a train whistle
sharpens the hour,
where my brother and I run
to the tracks
and line up pennies along the rail.
Day after day, we attend the iron clatter.
Once the train has passed,
we search the railroad ballast
for shine, filling pockets
with flattened coins
we will hide beneath doilies,
between couch cushions, in cracks
of the chimney's crumbling mortar.
Once I am older,
older than now, I will want
                              to live again
in a place I can discover things forgotten
so I might again
leave them where they are.

Hay Song

> *after Béla Bartók's Violin Duet No. 12*

An almost late season came
early through morning
frost and song of the alfalfa
near-bloom's violet &
                          reluctant unfolding.

Pale green stalk after stalk
cut and piled. She feeds
the sheep, singing, *Lord, look*
what has flowered,
                        or would have.

Eternal Cycle: A Child's Dream

When we wanted to play grown-ups,   my brother and I read
from our father's sleep studies, transcripts recording disturbances—

pages detailing tape tracks of traffic sounds,   bird calls, clicking
metronomes—and participants' dreams. My brother poured Legos

into metal bowls,   jumped with Moon Shoes on the bed, stuck
Playdough in my ears. I pretended to be the subject startled awake

and told my brother, the scientist,   *I dreamt only of gray towers.*
Summers at Gulf Shores, the two of us would gather beached jellyfish

bare-handed,   load our red wheelbarrow full of iridescent bodies,
and return them to sea. We watched frigate birds above the beach.

They did not stop.   They never do, even sleep wakeful. Running
with our wheelbarrow, we could be them, mimic their constant flight,

our thoughts of fish and daydreams. At night, our arms swollen
with rashes, we would cry   and refuse to sleep.

Still Life (An Offering)

Athena's hunt
turns to the rabbits
again—they've dug a hole
under the fence to graze
on clover in the yard
and lettuce from our garden.
Our cat stalks first, planning
the course of her attack,
chasing them through
kale and eggplant to a corner
where they halt, trapped.
Mornings, we open
the door wondering what
violence she will have
left us. Sometimes
I stop her. She claws
at my arms, bites my wrists.
She knows no rule but this:
to take what is defenseless
and drag it to the altar
of the porch steps,
its stillness her triumph.

The Amniocentesis

At the vineyard the winemaker shows us
the barrel thief, a glass tube,

>   a way of drawing out wine

>   to test its readiness,

>   and now I'm back

in my mother's womb, reaching for the needle's silver,
my first wound

>   still red years later

>   like sliced fruit I hold out

>   on my palm. For my mother,

a way to be sure—collecting the warm
water, my silent house—that I would

>   stand at the doorway

>   when she called my name.

>   And, when the need to be near

filled her throat, she knew I would reach
for what was close.

At World Market You and I Shop for a Living Room Carpet

I slide the rugs apart that are hanging

    from a line, and we stand

between the hooked and Balkan embroidered.

    I prefer those woven with colored silk

and, you, the beige sisal. We consider

    which would complement our oil-on-canvas

of Yellowstone Park's basin pools—

    dramatic Sunset Lake with its spill

of ground ginger and sumac,

    boiling thermophiles, meaning *heat*,

meaning *love*. You are tired of me

    showing you other people's homes

on Pinterest to prove how beautiful the blue will be

    beside the gold. I argue

for more flourish; you worry

    it would be too much. But when I walk

through a room, I want lotus flowers

    opening at the corners,

the tree of life bordering the wall,

    and peonies surrounding a bird.

Each image bright and distinct, repeated

        between columns of stars.

In the store, I trace with my eyes closed

        how it would unfurl on our floor—the buta

in alternating teardrops beneath our feet,

        the scalding at its center.

Eternal Cycle: Nomad's Dance

> *"Manoir des mes rêves," sometimes translated as "Castle of my dreams," is Django Reinhardt's symphony inspired by a dream he had about living in an infinite forest*

A single pink streak   sweeps the sky, lingering
light by which   I pitch my tent. I swing

and thread poles through   nylon loops.
Young sassafras trees   draw thin lines across

the darkening   horizon. Building a fire, I can barely
see outlines   of hammocks and campers

huddled like caravans—
           Django, is this the castle,
Manoir des mes rêves,   the past you dreamt of

that late winter in 1942,   when all your hand's fingers
could press upon   the guitar strings' pulse?

What song   is not a story? Pont-à-Celles' forest
of black pine,   the sound of violins around a fire,

your *roulotte* before paper   flowers surrendered
to the flame.   Wind stirs ashes in the air, snow

rising and settling   in my hair. When I fall asleep,
embers glow   within my eyes' dark chambers.

After You Died, I Looked for Your Poem

for Richard, Class of 2016

I wake. Poetry enters the body. Slice and pit
a peach. Poetry enters the body.
I put the kettle on for tea. Words enter me
across and through my hands that raise,
without prayer, the mug to my mouth.
Poem after poem suffers this space.
Some days having them is not enough.
Some days speaking them would be too much.

After you died, I looked for the poem you wrote
in 9th grade. I found essays, a test, a project.
You had covered every paper with stars—
stars dotting i's, pink stars, stars with squiggly lines
to give them their glow. I opened and closed
the same drawers for days
thinking I would find it, dust-covered,
crinkled at the corners. Some spaces are filled
with emptiness.

        Now, there are stacks of paper
on my classroom desk and floor.
                      I go to sleep
in that black sky of stone. Poem after
poem. I looked for you.

Anti-Elegy Before the First Frost

for Mary

The moon is a hole punched in the sky
by the time you arrive to help me cover

the garden before tonight's frost. I'm already
in the backyard bending poles into arches,

forcing tips into the dirt. As we walk
the rows of raised beds, floodlights flicker

in the dark, mantling young garlic & broccoli
with shine & umbra.

You point to the broken eggshells I've scattered
in the soil & say it reminds you

of your eldest daughter's first art installation:
shadow boxes filled with cracked tree swallow

& bluebird eggs, peppered rock-shield, apple moss,
goose feathers, a clouded sulphur butterfly

identified female by its wings' scalloped black edging.
You miss her, haven't kissed her forehead since

she crossed the Atlantic to visit you last spring.
I can't see it. In this dark,

I see white shatters, and, in flurried pointillism,
black flecks dart. I close

and rub my eyes. You shake out
the yards of gauzy fabric you've brought.

Holding opposite ends, we raise it high over
the planted plastic half-orbits. The fabric drapes

the breeze before it settles,
like a girl's skirt billowing as she descends

a flight of stairs, toward the earth, toward us.
The beds now sheltered in sheets, we tack down

the cloth corners to the wood. Tonight, I'll worry less
about what might die. I say you should stay

for dinner, *I'll make risotto with mushrooms and peas.*
Around us, in the gusty night air, ghost ships—risen

across the yard—drift away from our sight
as though they might yet reach some distant sea.

III

Soul Theory Cast in Bronze

In a life before   my mother's and mine, my grandmother
prepares our clay. I tell her,   *I want to pick*
the shapes: I cut my hands into a cathedral.
In the next room, a ribbon   smolders on a brazier, and, smelling
smoke, we press   hopefully against our empty
jewelry boxes, not yet   ready to be filled with stones.
There is a word that means   my body is my soul—
it rubs freckled paint   on my chest and has the scent
of a mower coursing   through a highway median
of wildflowers. When the molten   bronze is ready,
I pour liquid   into a molding, piece myself together
in a variety   of sizes—a medium casting
for a display in which   I am nude and impassioned,
a few small ones   in anguished poses for the Gates
of Hell, and a life-size   casting of me driving my car
through a military base   near Southern Pines.
Once the bronze sculptures' seams are cast,   I look heavy,
except the slim wrists   my grandmother shaped.
Stiff and hollow, I   watch a soldier, in rescue
simulation, resuscitate   a dummy. I stop my car
on the roadside, uncertain   how to save the soft fruit
enclosed in its husk.   The dummy empties its shell, lost
wax bleeding out   to harden in the sun.

Recollection Following a Rest

after Pat Martino's album Footprints

In the yellow light of his living

      room lamp, ever since

his aneurysm, the flags

      of the semiquaver rest look foreign—

the symbol's lack of hesitation,

      its slash tilted expectantly

toward the next note; he scratches

      the sheet music with his pen

in an attempt to remember

      how to write silence.

Once the song ends,

      he moves the needle

back to the record's

      rim and lowers it to again hear

himself as he was.

      The hollow

bass's double stops,

      in their unpredictability,

burst like red balloons

        underwater, in the brain,

into music.

        His blood stains the memory.

Through a reply

        that steps in black ink

through white space

        and the guitar's autumn

burst, he sits listening to his

        pickup's electric hum.

Winter

> *after Mot Studio's* Lesquatrestacions

There: my heartbeat
is that final violet circle,
        heavy with its music,

sloughing toward silence.
        The song, once blue

and teal blotches,
half-moons of green,

reaches its end. Once again
        winter's white plate.

Once again, this quiet

grows: tulip shoots
covered in snow.

Aubade from the Stokesville Country Store Parking Lot in February

Inside my car, as the frost turns to dew, I drink black coffee
        from a styrofoam cup

and watch two pigs in a field eat bugs from the grass.
        Inside the store, the clerk wraps

cinnamon rolls in plastic. Tonight, she will make a new
        batch, letting the dough rise

under a warm, damp towel her grandmother embroidered
        with daisies. She will again wake

before shadows grow slant from edges of stone, walk from
        her father's farmhouse

to the store, and when she turns on the light, she will
        close her eyes, turn her face

from the ceiling and back to the sky outside the open door,
        to the sun's slow ache.

Self-Portrait on the Surface of Someone Else

Wiping haze from the glazing on their faces,
removing sheets of dust from picture
frames' top edgings,
                      I think of how young

these people are—their stillness—of how soon
they might die, of how much I have
not meant for me:
                      my aunt's drawing

of her uncle. Friends are surprised
when they learn it is not a photograph.
They examine the creases around his eyes—

his wool hat and the soft shadows
it casts upon his brow—searching for proof
that it isn't an exact likeness,
                      but art.

Compared to the photograph I have of him,
he is slightly older, though unmistakably
the same man, the same weary

satisfaction in his eyes and mouth.
And his reserve, on which I blame my own
inability to make small talk.
                      Its title—

1991, the year my brother was born.
I like to think my aunt divined a connection
between his birth and this man's

finished portrait.
                Sometimes, I believe
it was meant to be my brother's inheritance.
Other days, I approach the drawing

and catch myself in its glass reflection.
Layered over the aging man,
                              there I am,
older than I ever imagined.

Imprinting

I was born with a mark on my palm
easily mistaken for a burn.
I have a filial affection for might-be flames
but ones I can touch
and take as mine: a mountain fire
bush's new leaves,
a Persian silk tree's fibrous blooms,

a red bulb to warm the quail eggs
that were hatched in a lab.
My father reared them, fed them
red cactus pear,
taught them what choices to make.
When offered cascara and assorted larva,
they hesitated at the lack of color.
Developing adaptive preferences from birth
he titled the paper.
His students broke the quails' necks,
plucked their scaled feathers for a feast,
ripping the birds' thin skin
in a rush to be rid
of their plumage.
                      Hypothesis:
I would make a beautiful feathered

creature. My mother, the microbiologist,
anatomized *Martha Stewart Living's* annual
Halloween edition,
Martha's Spooky Scary Sounds
screeching through the boombox.
To chimerical wailing and offbeat creaking,
I chose the most flammable:
an organza ghost,
a matador with her cape.
The year I was a raven,
I spray-painted my hair black.
The enamel webbed the strands inseparable.
My muslin feathers brushed
against walkways' paper lanterns lit dim

and dangerous. If my wings caught fire,
a bevy of hands palming
the grass for a hose slick and black in the dark
could only save what remained of me—
singed wire too heavy for flight.

Tat Tvam Asi (You Are That)

Ants track in and out of the punctures
in its trunk as the arborist inspects

the willow oak. These holes are different
from the signs that warn

of adelgid, which feed by inserting
their slender mouths through the bark—

he would know. The way I know
the soul fills and empties every

few years. Sap oozes from wounds
where someone once used climbing spikes

to scale its height. To remove the tree,
he would have to rent a crane. Better

it should stay—some limbs are less rotten
than we expect. The arborist

ascends to thin the canopy, swinging
from his pulley system, a saw

in hand. At a limb's knot, he finds
a callus and begins to prune, splintering

tissue beneath skin. What returned
in gaps I thought were injuries

again leaves me. He guides each
severed branch slowly to the ground.

Anti-Elegy with a Nine Iron in Its Hand

    for Dustin

I unhinge a cardinal from my cat's jaw,
object to her cull & feast as though she were not wild.

She watches its departure, rasps the air between
crimson feathers clinging to her gums.

Death is expected, though it happens more
some days than others. I've learned brightness

won't always be blood, though the sight of it
can deceive, wrench open small griefs,

like a Valentine polyester rose
blinking at its stamen, surviving on less than nothing.

*

I can't drive to work without being struck with shining—
the reflective vest strapped to a man

who walks down Lakeside Avenue,
a nine iron twirling in his right hand.

As he forges unharmed through the crosswalk,
a stoplight on this rainy morning

flushes red water rippling down glass
like the twenty ounces of Kool-Aid years ago

you placed in my car's cup holder. That day,
when I crashed into a utility pole,

your drink splattered the windshield & things rifled
from their places. An officer drew an aureola

across my pupils with his flashlight,
Both of you alright?

My eyes, unsteady in response, replayed the steel
cutter before it fractured

tempered glass. What more can I take
of that car than a torn scrap of headlight without its bulb.

I dug it from the mud
beneath a field of electrical wire humming,

deafening. I did not hear you speak again for years.
Yesterday, you called wanting to know how much color

had faded from my right shoulder blade's tattoo,
its fire dying from scarlet to rust.

When we crashed, I touched your arm.
It was so warm.

Looking Glass Falls

I go to the falls to see myself
in its glass, walk down the stone stairs
to where water touches water

loudly, but it's too late
in the morning—sunlight glints

where water bends—the ice
has melted from the rock,
and through the mist and rush,

I cannot find my face. Pebbles blur
in the shallow beneath my feet.
Pennies in a fountain. I wish to be

on its surface. Laurel grows crooked
from cracks in the rock. What abandon.

Eternal Cycle: A New Life

> *And all in war with Time for love of you,*
> *As he takes from you, I engraft you new.*
> *—Shakespeare, Sonnet 15*

When I consider everything that grows
holds its blossom but for a moment,

I think of tomato breeders surely wanting
the sweetest fruit. I think of all those

at war with rot, removing
one tomato's anther and brushing

its exposed stigma with another's pollen,
hoping, *This one will be better.*

With slices of Cherokee Purple
and Indigo Rose salted on my plate,

I think of the gardener who
will take from life to engraft a new—

the purple, the blue—drizzle them
with balsamic, and say, *They're perfect.*

*

They could have been perfect, she might think,
trimming off the tags—Sweet Sunrise—

the name that would have been
had they survived the late blight,

had she removed the diseased plants sooner,
been more diligent turning and tending

the compost, reviewed the horticulture textbook.
Next time, she will check young leaves twice

for spots, treat the soil with copper.
She feels foolish failing to recognize

the tomatoes' wilt for what it was—dying,
not thirst. It is late in the season

for seedlings. She is pulling,
pulling, the roots, stubborn & still holding.

Driving Past 8720 River Road on Christmas

I return to this house   of brightness.
A lifetime has been   passing. Santa still
waves from his sleigh, his reindeer mid-flight.
The elves haven't tired of making new toys.

Gingerbread men hold hands in a line;
across from them   golden rings overlap, inflatable
and blinking, next to penguins with eyelash extensions.
All the icicle lights.
                       What is the point of this,
with no child in the backseat of my car? I don't even want

                           to sing
a carol. Mostly, I am here to see
this house, full of brightness, to listen
to the speakers blare   *Oh Holy Night*.
Those turtle doves, and luminous pears. I forget
it's night,   the plastic carolers bathed
in white-yellow-white.

Eternal Cycle: Back to the Light

Some astronomer might be studying
the Trifid nebula, its infant stars' blue

light, the Earl Grey tea now cold
on her desk, when she first notices

the spacecraft's broadcast: a comet
close enough to see.

She calculates its orbit on the back
of an envelope she has been

meaning to take to the post office.
What is its albedo in comparison

to the Hall of Mirrors at Versailles?
she wonders to herself,

doodling Orion on the envelope's fold,
his shield full of stars.

*

Tonight is the brightest it will be.
I arrange a lawn chair to face Northwest,

ready for the stars to blink open,
wondering, *Will I see its light*

with just my eyes? My mother calls
to tell me she saw it on Sunday,

describes how NEOWISE glows,
how its trail of dust and melting snow

reminds her of a veil.
Leaning against the chair, my back

aching from the day,
I fall asleep waiting for the night

and dream of light somewhere in orbit—
drawn to and falling from the sun.

IV

Long Ago Was the Then Beginning to Seem Like Now

    after John Ashbery's "Blue Sonata"

I have never felt having too much   wanting
only enough   To let in more light

I twist open the blinds that hang like sheet
music   Between slat lines shines

a car's rear view mirror   A hammer
echoes   Workers continue repairing

the neighbor's roof   Yesterday I promised myself
today I was going to practice   Last month

Isou sent me her copy of Violin Sonata No. 5
As I flip through the pages   reading her penciled

markings   position shifts and fingerings
    I trace her slurs from note

to note   hills along the page   arcs like those
the tattoo artist in Italy drew   rising and falling

    a horizon of mountains along my arm
I can hear the machine's hum and pulse

as she pressed against my skin   inking the day
MaryAnne and I biked to San Marino

the chalk markings from the Giro d'Italia
    a cascade of color on the pavement

As we rode   we shouted the painted
words *vai vai!*   Wind furled

and unfurled flags atop Fortress Guaita   A tarp billows
across the street   A flock of birds lift from

a leaf pile   My bow in hand   I look at the song
before me   There is already so much music

Grocery Shopping After School

On my way home, I go to the store for rapini,
tomatoes, white beans. Walnuts and

blueberries. Cage free eggs are on sale. The best ones
are speckled brown and carefully handled.

I can't stop remembering class today

> and Grace, sleepy because her parents
> woke her early before school to hunt
>
> for Easter eggs. Cracking the plastic open cleanly,
> she shared what she had, chick- and egg-shaped
>
> treats. I imagine her with a wicker basket walking toward
> a light blue shape tucked into the boxwood.

All this bounty. This abundance of artichokes

and chives. I came for less than this. To check the fruit
for rot, I turn each piece twice over in my hand.

> I see it: Grace's parents sitting on the patio,
> watching her search the stems of daffodils
>
> and checkered lilies. Next to them a bowl
> of candies. They dare each other to eat a peep.

Repeating my list again in my head, I walk past
chocolate bunnies on display. I can picture

> having a child named Grace, waking her on
> a Monday because she spent Easter with her
>
> grandmother, and pointing her in the direction
> of pastel yellow, the curved edge of something
>
> breaching unraked leaves. What I can see
> or know has nothing to do with desire.

Rapini, tomatoes, white beans.... I think I have
probably forgotten something, like coffee

or bleach. I could get some just in case

but don't. This is enough—me with a basket in the bend
of my arm, waiting in line with what I've found.

Spring

While I chop onions and garlic,
I look outside my window:
succulents have sprouted from rocks,
mushrooms sprawl the wood pile
like cracked plates arranged along a stair.

My neighbor's daughter plays alone,
blowing bubbles in their yard.

Years ago, I would have thought
of need. Now, everything is becoming.
The field of it stretches beyond

my sight. Oil shimmers
in a pan. I scrape in the onion, wait
for it to brown. Approaching the glass pane,
bubbles shiver with gloss & open
at the slightest touch.

Eternal Cycle: A Peaceful Mind

You asked for the answers in French class; you knew
how to conjugate *être*—to be—but could not remember

that *tenir*—to hold, to keep—has the same pattern
as *étinceler*—to sparkle. I let you look over my shoulder

when you got up to sharpen your pencil, to see
that *vouloir*—to want—is the same as *savoir*—to know.

        For the Festival of Lights, we got matching
henna tattoos and ate your father's homemade samosas.

Your sisters danced. You knew every mudra: the fingers
pinched and splayed like a bird of paradise means

pulling the bow string. You showed me how hands
tell the story. *See, they are offering betel leaves.*

I watched sequins glint as the dancers held the shape
of a bowl—*lotus blooming*. What have I ever known?

Kenny Werner on the One-Finger Piano Exercise that Opens the Door to God

To practice the perfect drop,
I take the sheet music for "Balloons"

off the piano, lay it on the floor, and steady
my first finger over a white key.

Release to gravity.
                      Defy gravity.

The earth an anchor,

                    the heavens a crane.

A bird is known by the call it makes again
and again to another bird that replies

with the same sound. In the air, I sense
the remnants of a recent fire—the ash

                    of a thumb's rise

and fall. It is evening, and someone is clearing
the dinner table. A knife topples

from a stack of plates.

                    My bones lift.

Soft and light is the note singing
to an apartment across the hall.

I ready my hand for the second finger's fall.

The Volunteers

We've been working in the garden all morning,
planting the fickle Dark Galaxy tomatoes
prone to blossom-end rot.
Because you love the stripes of the universe
on your salads, I help you plant them anyway.
To make space in the beds, we must
first pluck the volunteers—cherry tomatoes
three inches tall, maybe a squash
or zucchini, and what I believe is a sweet potato,
purple heart-shaped spades conquering
leaf by leaf the plot in which it arrived.
They provide what wasn't on purpose,
and we save only what we desire: okra
for its red-white blooms and a few yellow chiles.

Falcon 9

for Josh

In alternating day and night shifts, you work at O'Hare, preparing the albatross. Outside the hangar, the hours choke with exhaust. Wearing, as always, your blue Dickies, you de-ice planes' wings each winter. How long it lingers—that scent of jet fuel in the fold of your cargo pockets. Last year, once the wind was less cruel and the ice cracked in plates on the surface of the Chicago River, you bought a camera to journal the rites foreshadowing spring. Those late winter weeks wake the same. Salt washing from the sidewalks. The Ferris wheel illuminated in stillness at Navy Pier. The camera brought you awe, burning among the constellations, my brother who never sees the stars. Our father thinks there should be more evenings ending in fireworks, but you've seen enough light falling into Lake Michigan. When Delta finally granted you three vacation days, you waited six hours on standby for a seat to LA. The night you walked along Hermosa Beach, a rocket launched—a prisoner's cinema of blown glass escaping to the sea—its contrail a gash on the horizon hours after you took the photograph. You had searched among skyscrapers for beauty; it arrived, beyond the high-rises, sudden and impermanent in a smoke line on the face of the sky. In an ocean that gave itself to fire.

Anti-Elegy with a Painter's Brush and a Bowl of Unripe Peaches

Because the fired clay has thawed
& cracked, water finds its way

between the chimney's bricks,
carrying salt from the mortar

to the plaster inside
my home. The wall blooms:

it molders & flowers into fleece
above the mantle, swelling

a map of the water's path.
Efflorescence, the same

misfortune Michelangelo
found in the chapel's damp

ceiling while painting *The Flood.*
When the sky blistered

and ochre pigments flaked
off the Ark, did he think

of the irony—of Noah
preparing for the deluge—

as he climbed the scaffolds
to restore the pillars & hull?

Last spring, once the birdbath
filled to its brim

and puddles collected
on the driveway, I cut away

plaster to scrub the chimney
with vinegar. Paint petals

fall again to the floor.
Outside, a peach tree drops

immature fruit for those more
ripe and healthy, & the weight

of a tiger lily's early bloom
pulls its stem into an arc.

Eternal Cycle: Terre des Hommes

Holding the cover of Wrembel's album,
      turning it over in my hand,
I remember I once doubted
      this man sketched on the insert
could survive so incomplete,
      thrust from the heavens,
an imperfect corpse of etches
      and half-bones. Though drawn
without ears, he hears a murmur
      within. He plays strings of slack keys
with every breath. Wind strums
      his ribcage, scratches across
his harp, the ghost note of one who,
      as the sun warms his back, is radiant
with light. He reaches
      without a hand to remove
the shard of glass buried in a heel
      that has no foot. So much is lost.
In his falling, he looks up,
      mouth open in wonder,
unaware of a landscape
      below him, rusted and barren.

Burial Mounds (The New Year)

The sun setting at our backs, we drag
your mother's tree out to the bay, fir needles

shedding along the sidewalk. Christmas trees
are piled at the beach entrance. Some, discarded

weeks ago, are amber now, thinning, nearly buried
in the dunes' eroding gowns. We pick an empty

spot beyond the wrack line where the wind stirs dried algae
and crab carcasses along the hard-packed shore.

On our return, you reach for my hand, gummed
and coarse with sand and resin. You know another

way—we walk past silver and blue ornaments
still hanging from a dogwood tree, take a shortcut

behind the cedar-sided cottage, our path
strung with lights that the neighbors left up.

Jessica Conley holds a BA in English, an MT in Secondary English Education, and an MFA in Poetry from Virginia Commonwealth University. She currently teaches at John Marshall High School. She is a Pushcart Prize nominated poet who has been published in literary magazines such as *Glassworks Magazine, Common Ground Review,* and *2River.* Jessica lives in Richmond, Virginia with her musician husband, John R. Conley. In her free time, she enjoys racing cyclocross and getting lost on the bike. You can visit her online at jessleeconley.com.

www.ingramcontent.com/pod-product-compliance
Lightning Source LLC
Chambersburg PA
CBHW030057170426
43197CB00010B/1566